Unleash the F Juicing

Everyday Juicer & Blender Recipes
With listed health benefits!

Table of Contents

Introduction — 4
Disclaimer — 6
Fruit Juice Recipes — 7
  The Super Booster — 7
  Berry Super-Fruits with a Mango Twist — 9
  Immunity Boost Juice — 11
  Tropical Paradise Juice — 13
  Pomegranate and Blackberry Breakfast Juice — 15
  Star fruit Surprise — 17
  Whole Fruit Juice — 19
  Water Melon and lime juice — 21
  Blueberries and Cantaloupe Juice — 22
  Honey and Guava Juice — 23
  Yellow Submarine — 25
  Golden Juice — 27
Vegetable Juice Recipes — 29
  The 1-2 Punch Green Veggie Mix — 29
  The Pepper Pick Me Upper — 31
  I see, You See Juice Mix — 33
  The Green Goddess — 35
  Eggplant Especial Juice — 36
  Healthy Evening Juice Mix — 37
  Pepper Juice — 39
  Blushing Carrots — 40
  Taste of Veggies — 42

Pepper Perfection	**44**
Veggie Delight	**46**
Vegetable and Fruit Juice Recipes	**47**
Looks Like Slime, But Tastes Like Heaven	**47**
The Green Monster	**49**
Fruit and Veggie Supreme	**51**
Green Monster Goo	**53**
Anytime Juice Mix	**55**
Wake me up and Go Juice	**56**
Homemade Berry Juice	**58**
Veggie Lemonade	**60**
Super Juice	**62**
Cucumber and Pears Galore	**64**
Apple Surprise	**66**
Beat the Heat	**68**
Conclusion	**70**

Introduction

Juicing is something that has been around for quite a while and is catching on pretty quickly. The health benefits associated with fresh juices are great and you can meet your daily nutritional needs with a drink that tastes really delicious. Fresh Juice not only helps your system detoxify, thereby making your brain work better, it helps your heart function optimally as well. When you start using these juicing recipes daily, you will likely start to see a marked improvement in your overall energy level and feel great. You may even consider taking up some sort of exercise routine in order to boost your overall health.

It is like the old saying goes: The fresher, the better! That is why I have put together this recipe book full of juices to meet your goal of creating a natural, homemade, preservatives and additives free drink. Some juices particularly target weight loss and some target cleansing, depending upon the ingredients. In the pages to follow, I will break the benefits down for you, as well as give you the best time to drink them such as morning or evening. However, it is not recommended to juice alone to lose weight as you need to eat also! It is the vitamins and the healthy benefits of the fruits and vegetables that help you lose weight, while still maintaining a healthy diet.

Also, try your best to make your juices from organic fruits and vegetables. Organic is the best for you and will provide the least amount of pesticide residue or other things of that nature. You can even grow your own fruits and vegetables for your juicing purposes. You probably won't be able to grow everything you eat, but you can grow a lot of ingredients in pots or in your own yard. That way you see them grow and know for sure there is nothing added to them that will cause any damage to your body.

Should you use a juicer or a blender??? The answer is: whatever you prefer will work with the recipes to follow. The recipes that follow are only basic recipes which have plenty of room to be modified according to your juicing or blending needs and according to the flavors you prefer. However, from my personal experience I have found that soft textured fruits that are not as juicy such as bananas are better suited for blender than a juicer. Same goes for leafy green vegetables that aren't as juicy but are added to juices for their nutritional benefits. Also, using leafy vegetables and soft textured fruits in blenders saves you from time consuming and inconvenient hand washing of juicer blade and filter grill. I can tell you from experience that it is not a lot of fun having to hand-wash the juicers' filter grill with a soft tooth brush in order to get the remains of leafy vegetables out. So unless you have a personal preference to use juicer for such fruits and vegetable, blender is the way to go for such recipes. For all other juicy fruits and vegetables such as carrots, apples, kiwis etc a juicer is the best option but again the choice lies with you. So go with your preference and these basic recipes to create as many delicious juices as you can think of. Drink healthy and be happy!!!!

Disclaimer

All rights Reserved. No part of this publication or the information in it may be quoted from or reproduced in any form by means such as printing, scanning, photocopying or otherwise without prior written permission of the copyright holder.

Disclaimer and Terms of Use: Effort has been made to ensure that the information in this book is accurate and complete, however, the author and the publisher do not warrant the accuracy of the information, text and graphics contained within the book due to the rapidly changing nature of science, research, known and unknown facts and internet. This book is not meant to be taken as medical advice and consists only of the benefits that have been long known and shown by various research studies to be beneficial for human body. As always, before making any drastic changes to your regular diet or starting a special diet plan, refer to your physician for advice. The Author and the publisher do not hold any responsibility for errors, omissions or contrary interpretation of the subject matter herein. This book is presented solely for motivational and informational purposes only.

Copyright © 2014 by Sarah Reed

All Rights Reserved Worldwide

Fruit Juice Recipes

The Super Booster

Ingredients:

1 Apple

1 and 1/2 Pears

2 Kiwis

5 Cherries (pitted)

(Serves 1)

Directions:

1. Cut the apple, pears and the kiwis into slices
2. Add the cherries
3. Place all the fruits in the blender and blend if you prefer juices with fruit pulp and a slight thicker consistency. Otherwise, run all fruits through a juicer.
4. Pour the fresh juice into a glass and serve.

Apples contain a particular kind of flavonoid which is known to be only found in apples. This compound can protect bones against osteoporosis. In addition to being loaded with vitamin C and K to fight free radicals and improve the immune system health, pears are also a high fiber fruit that can improve heart health. In addition to their beautiful green color, Kiwis are full of fiber and phytonutrients which can help repair damaged DNA. Cherries contain a compound known as anthocyanin, which is a type of anti-inflammatory natural pain reliever.

This fruit juice mixture makes a great breakfast, packed full of vitamins C and E and other healthy properties, this juice will start your morning off right.

Berry Super-Fruits with a Mango Twist

Ingredients:

1 cup blueberries

1/2 mango

1 cup strawberries

1 whole pomegranate

(Serves 1)

Directions:

1. Cut the mango into slices
2. Peel pomegranate and preferably separate seeds from the skin as leaving the skin on can result in a bitter taste.
3. Run all the fruits through the juicer for pulp and seed free juice. A blender can be used if fruit pulp is preferred in the juice.
4. Pour the fresh juice into a glass and serve fresh.

Pomegranate is packed with heart healthy antioxidants that keep the bad cholesterol (LDL) in check and prevent the hardening of the arteries. Blueberries are also a heart healthy fruit but are good for eyes as well. Recent studies have shown that blueberries have compounds that are similar to cranberries and can not only prevent but cure the urinary tract infection as well. Mango is a very goo source of potassium which can help control hypertension. Strawberries are packed with compounds known as polyphenols which can remove the free radicals and boost the immune system.

This antioxidant rich juice will boost your day with the use of all "super fruits," and it makes a great lunch juice.

Immunity Boost Juice

Ingredients:

1 orange

1 grapefruit

3 kiwis

1 cup strawberries

(Serves 1)

Directions:

1. Peel the orange and the grapefruit
2. Cut the orange, grapefruit and kiwis into slices
3. Add the strawberries
4. Run all the fruits through the juicer for a pulp free drink or use a blender if thick consistency of juice with pulp is preferred.
5. Pour the fresh juice into a glass and serve fresh.

Grapefruit is very high in vitamin C and phytonutrients known to fight disease and give the immune system a boost. It has also shown to be an effective fat burner and helps with weight loss. Oranges are not only packed with vitamin C but they are also high in fiber and improve health of the circulatory system including the heart. Kiwis are not only high in vitamin C but also contain many essential minerals such as iron and potassium needed for heart health.

High levels of vitamin C and antioxidants make this a great juicer mix for if you feel you are coming down with a cold. Remember to leave all your ingredients whole, you want to get the benefits of the skins.

Tropical Paradise Juice

Ingredients:

    1/2 pineapple

    1 mango

    1 orange

    (Serves 1)

Directions:

1. Peel the mango, orange and pineapple
2. Cut the fruit into manageable chunks
3. Run all the fruits through the juicer or blender if preferred.
4. Pour the fresh juice into a glass and serve fresh.

Sometimes I like to add strawberries or kiwi to this recipe, but this is the basic Tropical Paradise recipe

Pineapples have a natural digestive enzyme, called bromelain, that helps to rid your stomach of bad bacteria and they are high in vitamins C, A and B-complex. Mango has a mixture of vitamin A and C, along with antioxidants, enzymes and minerals that help to detoxify your body. Mangos are also known to improve the appearance of your skin. Oranges are packed full of vitamins C which boosts your immune system. Oranges also have vitamin A which is needed for eye health. All of these fruits work together synergistically to make you feel great overall!

Pomegranate and Blackberry Breakfast Juice

Ingredients:

1 pomegranate

1 cup blackberries

1 cup blueberries

1 banana

(Serves 1)

Directions:

1. Peel the pomegranate and the banana and cut them into small pieces.
2. Add bananas and pomegranate seeds into the blender along with the berries.
3. Place all the fruits in the blender and run it till a semi-smooth texture is achieved.
4. Pour the fresh juice into a glass and serve with ice.

Apart from the unique and pleasing flavor, pomegranates are also rich in antioxidants such as polyphenols which have disease fighting characteristics as they remove the free radicals. Pomegranates are also highly packed with anthocyanins which are natural anti-inflammatory pain relievers. These help in stimulating the blood flow to the heart while at the same time protecting against prostate cancer.

Have this juice mix with your morning routine and you will be sure to start your day off on the right foot!

Star fruit Surprise

Ingredients:

2 star fruit (also known as carambola)

3 kiwi

1 apple

1 1" slice of ginger

(Serves 1)

Directions:

1. Peel all the fruits and cut into manageable slices.
2. Run all the fruits and ginger through the juicer or blender if pulp or a thicker consistency is desired.
3. Pour the fresh juice into a glass and serve chilled.

Star fruit is packed with ascorbic acid which is needed for bone and mucous membranes health. It also contains beta-carotenes which are essential for eye health. Kiwis are not only high in vitamin C but also contain many essential minerals such as iron and potassium needed for heart health. Apples are high in fiber and packed with phytonutrients that are needed for a healthy body. Ginger has cancer fighting properties and research has shown ginger to fight ovarian and colon cancer cells.

Have this juice mix any time of the day or night, it will boost your immune system and assist with healing.

Whole Fruit Juice

Ingredients:

Half Pineapple

1 medium sized orange

1 medium sized banana

1 apple (large)

1 cup strawberries (fresh or frozen)

1 cup of seedless grapes

4 tablespoon honey

Ice (as needed)

(serves 6)

Directions:

1. Start by peeling off the pineapple and slicing them into small pieces.
2. Peel off the orange and the banana.
3. Peel off the apple and slice it.
4. Throw in all the fruits into the blender and blend to mix all the fruits together. (This recipe can be modified for juicer by omitting the banana.)
5. If the mixture is too runny then add some ice to it cautiously so that it does not become too thick.

6. Pour the fresh juice into a glass and savor the delicious tropical flavors.

As previously stated, pineapple, oranges and berries are loaded with vitamin C for immune system health and grapes also contain high amounts of vitamin C, K, and B6. Bananas are high in sugar and also have highest amount of vitamin K to be known in a fruit which is plays a key role in maintaining blood pressure. Honey has been known for years to have healing powers such as soothing irritated throat and coughing and improving gastro-intestinal health.

This delicious whole fruit juice consists of about 160 calories per glass and can serve as an ideal substitute for your breakfast as well. An addition of a scoop of your favorite protein powder to this recipe can also keep you energized and full longer.

Water Melon and lime juice

Ingredients:

¼ of a fresh watermelon approx. 2 cups (Seedless if available)

½ lime (juiced)

Ice (optional)

(serves 2)

Directions:

1. Start by slicing the watermelon into small pieces and remove all the seeds from it. (unless using the seedless watermelon)
2. Throw the watermelon into the blender and add lime juice to it. Watermelon can be run through the juicer if pulp free juice is preferred.
3. If the juice is too runny, add ice to the blender to make the texture a bit thick.

The watermelon and lime juice contains approximately 98 calories and is as an ideal snack for those who are trying to lose weight. Also it is rich in Vitamin A, C and B-6 thus helping you in boosting your immune system.

Blueberries and Cantaloupe Juice

Ingredients:

    1 cup blueberries (fresh)

    ½ cantaloupe

    3 apples

    Ice (optional)

    (serves 3)

Directions:

1. Start by removing the rind from the cantaloupe.
2. Peel and core the apples
3. Put all the fruits through a juicer or blender if thick consistency or pulp in the juice is desired.
4. Add ice and serve chilled.

    The blue berries and cantaloupe juice is rich in both Vitamin A and C and is an ideal morning delight. Additionally, cantaloupe alone is considered to be packed with potassium, Vitamins A, B1, B3, B6, C and K along with magnesium, fiber and folate.

Honey and Guava Juice

Ingredients:

1 medium sized guava

½ cup of water (cold)

3 teaspoons of honey

(serves 1)

Directions:

1. Wash the guava, deseed it and slice it in halves.
2. Throw the guava and water into the blender and blend.
3. Mix with honey and serve fresh.

Variation:

If this juice is to be made using a juicer then guava deseeding step can be skipped as the juicer will filter out the seeds from getting into the drink. However, guavas are not ultra juicy fruits so for juicer, a base fruit will be needed to provide the main liquid and water can be omitted. Apples, oranges, or strawberries can be a great addition if this recipe was to be made using a juicer.

The Guava and Honey juice is low in calorie and high in fiber thus proving to be an excellent option especially if you're trying to lose weight. Guava is also considered as the power house of nutrients. It is not only rich in proteins, vitamins, minerals and essential fibers but also contains zero cholesterol and has a rather amazingly low count of the digestible carbohydrates. This tropical fruit is also great for clear skin and gastro-intestinal health.

Yellow Submarine

Ingredients:

1 cup pineapple chunks

1 lemon (juiced if using blender)

½ tsp. stevia or honey (optional)

(Serves 1)

Directions:

1. If the pineapple is not already cut up, then you should cut up enough chunks to measure 1 cup.
2. Take the lemon next and cut it up into halves so that it can fit into the juicer. You can hand squeeze the juice of 1 lemon if you intend to use a blender for this recipe as entire lemon to the blender would lead to bitter taste. However, you can save the lemon skin and add some lemon zest to your juice if you desire.
3. Place all of the ingredients into the juicer or blender and turn it on high. Let the ingredients mix for about a minute so that they can become well combined.
4. Pour into a glass and enjoy.

Note: Pineapple and lemon together can be very sour and if your taste buds are not up for it, the option of adding natural, calorie free stevia or some honey to bring down the sourness is also available.

The Yellow Submarine consists of only 82 calories. This rich in protein juice is ideal for those who are conscious about their weight and are mindful about what goes in their body. Pineapples; one of the key ingredients in this juice is well known for containing bromelain which is a type of an enzyme that reduces inflammation and helps with your arthritis. Also, this exotic fruit is an excellent source of Vitamin C and assists in strengthening one's immune system. Addition of lemon which contains citric acid assists with the weight loss especially if taken at breakfast.

Golden Juice

Ingredients:

1 banana

3 to 4 oranges or ½ cup orange juice

2 kiwis

½ cup mango chunks

(Serves 1-2)

Directions:

1. To start this recipe, you will want to take the kiwis and peel the skin off them.
2. Place the kiwis into the juicer or blender before continuing.
3. Next take the banana and peel it before placing it along with the oranges and mango chunks into the blender. (bananas can be omitted if recipes is to be made in a juicer)
4. Turn the blender on and allow all of the ingredients to mix together until well combined.
5. When all of the ingredients are well combined, you can turn off the blender and pour the juice into a glass. Add in some ice before serving right away.

The Golden Juice is an absolute must for all the fitness freaks out there. As you know, bananas are well known for its high potassium content helpful in maintaining hypertension. Oranges and kiwis are full of vitamin C and mangos have high amount of vitamin A which is good for eye and bone health. This not only assists in your nerve and muscle function but at the same time also prevents from those rather painful muscle cramps after workouts.

Vegetable Juice Recipes

The 1-2 Punch Green Veggie Mix

Ingredients:

    1 small cucumber (peeled if preferred)

    1 or 2 stalks of celery

    5-6 Brussels sprouts (bottom stems cut off)

    1 red capsicum or bell pepper (cut and deseeded)

    1 & 1/2 cloves of garlic

    Pinch of salt (optional)

    Pinch of black pepper (optional)

    (Serves 2)

Directions:

1. Place all the veggies into your blender.
2. Blend until smooth and creamy
3. Add a pinch of salt and/or pepper to enhance the sweetness of vegetables. However, this is a completely optional step.
4. Pour in a glass and serve as a great juice for maintaining good health.

The base vegetables of this recipe will set you off with a blast of electrolytes and nutrients, while the other ingredients work their own magic. Brussels sprouts are known as one of the healthiest foods on the planet, but how frequently do you get a chance to have some? Brussels sprouts protect our DNA from damage with certain chemical compounds found in them; they also help to lower cholesterol. The natural healing ability of capsicum is that of a pain reliever, when applied topically, and it helps to boost your metabolism when ingested. Cucumbers mainly consist of water and are an excellent resource for keeping yourself naturally hydrated. Celery can be a great ingredient in this juice that helps in replenishing electrolytes lost after a hard work-out session.

The Pepper Pick Me Upper

Ingredients:

- 1 large bell pepper
- 2 stalks of celery
- 1 cucumber
- 1 carrot
- 1/2 cup eggplant – (with the skin left on if preferred)
- 1/2 handful basil
- 1/2 handful cilantro
- Pinch of salt & black pepper (optional)

(Serves 2)

Directions:

1. Chop all the vegetables into manageable chunks
2. Place all the veggies into your blender
3. Blend until smooth and creamy.

Note: Sometimes the cilantro can lessen the spicy effect, so if you want you can add extra pepper flakes and/or salt to give the juice a little kick.

Bell peppers have lots of vitamin C as well as other phytochemicals that protect your body with their antioxidant properties. Celery is a naturally calming vegetable, due to the minerals contained, magnesium in particular. The nervous system is quieted down by the stimulation celery provides. Cucumbers are a great source of B vitamins, which will give you energy to make it through your day. Carrots contain high levels of vitamin A, which helps with eye health, and they help maintain cardiovascular health. Eggplants contain phytonutrients that improve your blood circulation. Basil is said to contain anti aging properties as the antioxidants present in it kill off free radicals. Cilantro contains heavy metal bonding agents which aid in removing dangerous heavy metals from your body.

I see, You See Juice Mix

Ingredients:

   2 carrots

   1 stalk of celery

   1 tomato

   1 handful of parsley

   Pinch of salt & black pepper (optional)

   (Serves 1)

Directions:

1. Chop all the vegetables into manageable chunks
2. Place into your blender or juicer. (recipe can be modified for juicer by omitting cilantro)
3. Blend until smooth and creamy.
4. Add a pinch of salt and black pepper if desired. Serve chilled.

Carrots contain high levels of vitamin A, which helps with eye health, and they help maintain cardiovascular health. Celery contains minerals, magnesium in particular, that helps improve your nervous system function and can even give you a feeling of calm. Tomatoes have lots of vitamins and minerals such as vitamins A, C, K, B6 and magnesium, phosphorus and copper which all work together to maintain health. Parsley has vitamins C,

B-12, A and K that help you maintain a healthy body. Parsley also supports kidney function by helping to flush excess fluid from the kidneys. This is a great evening or afternoon juice mix. This juice will help you to relax and mull over the day.

The Green Goddess

Ingredients:

    5 leaves of romaine lettuce

    2 cups green cabbage

    2 carrots

    1 handful cilantro

    Pinch of salt & black pepper   (optional)

(Serves 2-3)

Directions:

1. Chop the cabbage and the carrot into manageable chunks.
2. Place into your blender.
3. Blend until smooth and creamy.
4. Add pinch of salt and pepper if desired and serve.

    Romaine lettuce has protein that is good for muscle development and repair, as well as being rich in B vitamins to give you energy. Cabbage is a great source for foliates, as well as vitamins C and K. Cabbage supports healthy bone structure and a healthy immune system. Carrots contain high levels of vitamin A, which helps with eye health, and they help maintain cardiovascular health. Cilantro contains heavy metal bonding agents that aid in removing dangerous heavy metals from your body.

Eggplant Especial Juice

Ingredients:

    1/2 Eggplant (unpeeled if desired)

    8-9 Brussels sprouts

    1 cup cabbage

    Pinch of salt & black pepper (optional)

(Serves 2)

Directions:

1. Place all vegetables into your blender.
2. Blend until smooth and creamy.
3. Add salt and black pepper if desired and serve chilled.

Add pinch of salt and/or pepper flakes as desired for any extra flavoring. Eggplants contain phytonutrients that improve your blood circulation. Brussels sprouts protect our DNA from damage with certain chemical compounds found in them and they also help to lower cholesterol. Cabbage is a great source for folates, as well as vitamins C and K. Cabbage supports healthy bone structure and a healthy immune system. You can have this power packed juice any time of day, and reap great health benefits of juicing.

Healthy Evening Juice Mix

Ingredients:

    1 handful spinach

    1 celery stalk (cut into chunks)

    2 tomatoes (sliced)

    1 handful grated ginger root (peeled)

    Pinch of salt & Pepper

    (Serves 1)

Directions:

1. Place all vegetables into your blender.
2. Blend until smooth and creamy.
3. Add a pinch of salt and/or black pepper if desired and serve chilled.

    Spinach promotes healthy brain function, thanks to the abundance of vitamin K found in spinach. Studies have shown that Spinach the most effectively absorbed by our bodies in the juice form. Celery contains minerals, magnesium in particular, that help improve your nervous system function and can even give you a feeling of calm. Tomatoes have lots of vitamins and minerals such as vitamins A, C, K, B6 and magnesium, phosphorus and copper which all work together to maintain health. Ginger works with all of the components of the juice to help your body better absorb all of the vitamins and nutrients.

Keep this juice recipe handy for the end of a long day or have right before a large dinner, if you are trying to lose weight.

Pepper Juice

Ingredients:

1 red bell pepper (seeds removed)

1 green bell pepper (seeds removed)

½ cucumber

3 stalks of celery

5 leaves of lettuce

Pinch of salt (optional)

(Serves 1)

Directions:

1. Take the two peppers, celery, cucumber, and the lettuce and cut them up into smaller pieces to make sure that they are small enough to fit into the blender.
2. Place the ingredients into the blender and let them blend until done.
3. Add a pinch of salt if desired and serve.

The Pepper Juice ranks quite high in protein and consists of only 97 calories per serving. Pepper; a base component in this juice is said to have antioxidant abilities which not only neutralize the free radicals in your body but also prevent the body from any symptoms of cell damage.

Blushing Carrots

Ingredients:

1 beet (peeled)

4 carrots

4 spinach leaves

6 Romaine leaves

(Serves 1)

Directions:

1. Take the carrots and the beet and cut it up into small pieces.
2. Next you can take the Romaine leaves and the spinach leaves, bunch them all up to give them a rough chop.
3. Place all of the ingredients into the blender and blend all of them together until done. This recipe can be modified for juicer by omitting the leafy vegetables.
4. Pour out into a glass and enjoy.

Carrots are one of the best nutritional supplements that a dieters and athletes can include in his/her diet. These are not only rich in potassium, fiber and minerals but are also packed with an abundant supply of vitamins; especially vitamin A which is good for your teeth and bones. Beets are a good source of folates and are especially beneficial for women who are expecting. These tubers are also high on beta carotenes which are essential for eye and heart health. Beets are especially beneficial for liver damage and have been known for years for their sexual health improving benefits.

Taste of Veggies

Ingredients:

1 celery stalk

1 beet

1 handful of parsley and spinach

1 green bell pepper

1 ginger slice

3 garlic cloves

4 carrots

(Serves 2)

Directions

1. For this recipe, you will want to take the celery stalk, beet, green pepper, and carrots and cut them up into smaller pieces. This makes them easier to fit into the blender.
2. Next, place the celery stalk, beet, spinach, parsley, green pepper, ginger, garlic clove, and carrots into your blender.
3. Cover the blender and blend all of these ingredients mixed together until they are well combined.
4. When the ingredients are ready, pour the mixture out into one of your favorite glasses.
5. Add in some ice if you would like to cool it down. Serve this juice right away.

The taste of veggies is an excellent alternative to your calorie packed breakfast. Moreover, it not only keeps your stomach full but the combination of beet, spinach, carrot, pepper and ginger equips your body with just the right amount of vitamins.

Pepper Perfection

Ingredients:

1 cucumber

1 red bell pepper

1 broccoli bunch

2 celery stalks

1 carrot

½ lime

1 handful of basil

½ cup Jicama

Tabasco sauce

(Serves 1)

Directions:

1. This recipe is perfect if you are looking to add in a little bit of spice and pepper to your day. To start this recipe, take the bell pepper, cucumber, broccoli, carrot, and the celery and place them into the blender or juicer.
2. When you are done blending or juicing these vegetables, make sure to set the juices aside for later.
3. You can then cut up the lime and the Jicama and save the other halves of them for later.

4. Place those two ingredients along with the basil and the Tabasco sauce into the blender. (Basil can be omitted to modify the recipe for a juicer.)
5. When everything has gone through the juicer or blender, combine together the juices of all the ingredients. Pour over some ice in a glass and serve.

This is undoubtedly one of the best vegetable juices that you can include in your diet. Packed with power vegetables like bell pepper, broccoli, lime, carrots and cucumber, this juice consists of only 88 calories and 10 grams of protein in just one glass. It is also rich in vitamins A, B, C and D along with a high content of Calcium, Magnesium and Potassium. Cucumber which is one of the base ingredients is well known for rehydrating your body while the sterols present in it aid in reducing bad cholesterol in your blood.

Veggie Delight

Ingredients:

1 piece ginger

2 carrots

1 lemon

1 cucumber

5 celery stalks

½ beet

(Serves 2)

Directions:

1. Take the carrots, cucumber, beet, and celery stalks and cut them up into smaller pieces.
2. Once that is done, you can bring out the blender and place all of the ingredients inside.
3. Blend these ingredients until everything is well combined and smooth.
4. Pour into a glass and then enjoy.

This exquisite combination of some of the healthiest vegetables that one could get their hands on is a must try for everyone. Just try having this juice twice a day and you will instantly start staying more energized reinvigorated and healthy during the day.

Vegetable and Fruit Juice Recipes

Looks Like Slime, But Tastes Like Heaven

Ingredients:

    3 stalks of celery

    1/3 of an Telegraph or English cucumber

    2 chard leaves

    1 pear

    1 apple

    Small handful of cilantro

    (Serves 2-3)

Directions:

1. For this recipe, you will want to take the celery stalk, cucumber, pear, and apple and cut them up into smaller pieces. This makes them easier to fit into the blender.
2. Next, place the ingredients into your blender or juicer. (Recipe can be modified for juicer by omission of leafy vegetables)
3. Add the chard leaves and cilantro for a blender recipe.
4. Cover the blender and all of these ingredients mix together until they are well combined.

5. When the ingredients are ready, pour the mixture out into one of your favorite glasses. Add in some ice if you would like to cool it down. Serve this juice right away.

Ginger is an option for flavoring this juice blend. Tailor it to fit your taste. You also have an option to leave the skin on all fruits and vegetables placed in your juicer if you wish to reap complete nutritional benefits of the ingredients.

The celery in the juice actually has a calming effect on the body, because of some of the minerals in celery, magnesium in particular. Celery can help free your body from heavy minerals. Cucumbers have been shown to have a vast amount of healthy properties, as well, including antioxidants that help fight cancer. They have a high amount of B vitamins, which will provide you with energy. Pears also offer antioxidants and they also aid in regulating blood pressure. Apples are a great source of fiber, and offer up tons of vitamin C.

The Green Monster

Ingredients:

    1 and 1/2 cucumber

    2 celery stalks

    1 kale leaf

    1 green apple

    1/2 lemon

    (Serves 1)

Directions:

1. For this recipe, you will want to take the celery stalk, cucumber and apple and cut them up into smaller pieces. This makes them easier to fit into the blender. By omitting the kale leaf, the recipe can be modified for a juicer.
2. Next, add the kale leaf and squeeze the lemon onto the mixture.
3. Place the ingredients into your blender or run all the ingredients through the juicer.
4. If using the blender then cover the top and blend all of these ingredients together until they are well combined.
5. Add in some ice and serve this juice right away.

    Cucumbers are a natural diuretic, meaning they help your body expel excess fluid and ridding you of that bloated feeling. Celery contains minerals, magnesium in particular, that helps improve your nervous system function and can even give you a feeling of calm. Kale has great anti-inflammatory properties and is high in both vitamin K and iron, as well as vitamins A and C. Green apples are great for digestion, as they are a good source of fiber, green apples also help regulate sugar levels in your body. Lemons are a powerful digestive aid, and the high levels of vitamin C in this citrus wonder helps to boost your immune system too. This juice mix will aid in digestion and any bloating issues you may be having. Nobody likes that feeling, so keep this recipe on hand for whenever you need it.

Fruit and Veggie Supreme

Ingredients:

    2 carrots

    1 tomato

    1 and 1/2 cup strawberries

    1 red apple

    1 piece of fresh ginger (optional)

    (Serves 2)

Directions:

1. Start off with dicing the carrots, tomato and the apple into manageable pieces. This makes them easier to fit into the blender or juicer.
2. Next, throw all the ingredients including strawberries and ginger into your blender or run through thc juicer.
3. Cover the blender and all of these ingredients mix together until they are well combined.
4. When the ingredients are well blended and are of the desired consistency, pour the mixture out from the blender.
5. Add in some ice if you would like to cool it down. Serve this juice right away.

    Because not everybody likes the taste of ginger, it can be optional for this recipe. Be sure to leave all fruits and vegetables whole when mixing up your juice.

Carrots have a lot of natural healthy properties, including vitamin A, which helps with your eyesight, and beta-carotene which aids in slowing the aging process with the multitude of anti oxidants carrots have. Tomatoes have lots of vitamins and minerals such as vitamins A, C, K, B6 and magnesium, phosphorus and copper which all work to maintain health. Strawberries have lots of antioxidants that help to protect the body from free radicals and stave off disease while providing a large dose of vitamin C. Red apples contain fiber, aiding in digestion, and studies have shown that eating 5 apples per week can help stave off respiratory problems. Ginger improves the absorption of vitamins and minerals, so if you like the taste it is a great additive to any juice recipe.

Green Monster Goo

Ingredients:

    1 handful fresh spinach

    1 and 1/2 stalks celery

    3 carrots

    1 apple

    1 handful parsley

(Serves 2-3)

Method:

1. Cut up the apples and the carrots, celery and spinach along with the parsley if you think that your blender can't handle them.
2. Place each of the ingredients into the juicer or blender one at a time and let them be juiced. Spinach and parsley can be left out to modify this recipe for a juicer.
3. Combine together the juices from all of the ingredients and mix well before enjoying.

    Spinach promotes healthy brain function, thanks to the abundance of vitamin K found in spinach. Studies have shown that Spinach the most effectively absorbed by our bodies in the juice form. Celery is a naturally calming vegetable, due to the minerals contained, magnesium in particular. Carrots contain high levels of vitamin A, which helps with eye health, and they help maintain cardiovascular health. Apples are good for the digestive system because of their fiber content, but they also contain vitamins C and B-6 which boots immunity and energy level as well. Parsley has vitamins C, B-12, A and K that help you maintain a healthy body. Parsley also supports kidney function by helping to flush excess fluid from the kidneys. This is a great lunch time shake. It will get you back on track for the rest of your busy day.

Anytime Juice Mix

Ingredients:

1 orange

1 cup blackberries

1 handful spinach

1 lemon

(Serves 1)

Method:

1. Place each of the ingredients into the blender or juicer one at a time and let them be juiced.
2. Combine together the juices from all of the ingredients and mix well
3. Serve chilled in one of your favorite glasses.

You can have this juice as a boost, or a pick-me-up any time of day.

Oranges are packed full of vitamins C, so they boost your immune system. They also have plenty of vitamin A needed for eye health. Blackberries are one of nature's healthiest berries, and because they are high in fiber blackberries aid in digestion and promote a high metabolism. Spinach promotes healthy brain function, thanks to the abundance of vitamin K found in it. Lemons are a powerful digestive aid, and the high levels of vitamin C in this citrus wonder helps to boost your immune system too.

Wake me up and Go Juice

Ingredients:

1 grapefruit (skinned and sliced in half)

1 cup of strawberries

1 cucumber

1 sprig of mint leaves

(Serves 1)

Method:

1. Place each of the ingredients into the juicer or blender one at a time and let them be juiced.
2. Combine together the juices from all of the ingredients and mix well
3. Serve chilled in one of your favorite glasses.

Grapefruits are a wonder fruit packed with vitamin C. Grapefruits aid in pain from arthritis and help lower the cholesterol. Strawberries are a great immune booster as they are packed with antioxidants and vitamin C. Cucumbers have been shown to have a vast amount of healthy properties, as well, including antioxidants that help fight cancer, and they have a high amount of B vitamins, which will provide you with energy. Mint leaves you feeling energized and awake, as well as helps to soothe stomach aches and cramps. Mint leaves even help pregnant women who are experiencing morning sickness. Drink this juice mix early in the morning during your normal routine for a day full of energy and refreshing positivity.

Homemade Berry Juice

Ingredients:

1 and ½ cups blueberries

1 cup beet greens

½ cup beets, sliced

½ cup cucumber, sliced

1 cup pineapple

1 cup celery

1 apple

1 cup kale, chopped

(Serves 1)

Directions:

1. To get started on this recipe, you need to take all of the fruits and vegetables and chop them up into smaller pieces. This allows them to fit into the blender or go through a juicer a little easier.
2. Next, place all of your ingredients into the blender before covering and turning the speed on high. Leafy vegetables can be omitted if a juicer is to be used.
3. When all of the ingredients are well combined, you can turn off the blender, bring out your

favorite serving glass, and pour the juice in. Serve with a little ice if desired.

Blue Berries; the key ingredient of this juice recipe tend to have the most amount of antioxidants in them. These are typically your free radical fighting power houses which boost your immune system. They are also quite rich in vitamin C and fiber. The Berry Juice serves as an ideal midday snack, restoring all the essential nutrients in your body allowing you to stay on top of your game.

Veggie Lemonade

Ingredients:

½ lemon

4 carrots

1 wedge red cabbage

1 apple

1 ginger round

(Serves 1)

Directions:

1. To start this recipe you will want to cut up the lemon in half and save the other part for later. Hand-squeeze one half of the lemon and keep on the side for later use.
2. Next cut up the carrots, get the right amount of cabbage, and core and cut up the apple. This will make it a lot easier to place these ingredients into the blender or juicer.
3. Run all these ingredients through the juicer or blend in the blender.
4. Add the ½ lemon juice to the mixture and serve right away.

The raw cabbage used in this juice consists of high amount of antioxidants and has immune boosting properties. It is also rich in fiber, mineral and vitamin C thus curbing any potential risks of cancer, diabetes, stroke and kidney stones. The Vegetable Lemonade is an absolute delight and works wonders alongside your low calorie dinner. Having just 65 calories itself, it restores all the essential nutrients back in your body that you lose during the hustle and bustle at work.

Super Juice

Ingredients:

1 beet

4 kale leaves

1 piece of ginger

1 lemon

1 apple

(Serves 1)

Directions:

1. To start this recipe take the peel and cut apples before chopping into smaller pieces.
2. Now hand-squeeze the lemon and keep the juice on the side for later use.
3. Once that is done, you can cut up the beet and bunch up the kale leaves before placing them along with the rest of the ingredients into the blender and covering it up. For juicer modification, kale leaves can be omitted or replaced with 1 cup of carrots.
4. Turn on the blender and let it go until the ingredients are combined and smooth or run the ingredients through a juicer.
5. Pour this juice into your favorite cup along with some ice. Serve this juice while it is still fresh.

The super juice is an excellent pre-workout juice, especially on those awfully tiring days when you just feel like you have no energy left in you to hit the gym. Also, it contains only 96 calories and 3 grams of proteins giving you just what you need to feel the motivation running through your veins.

Cucumber and Pears Galore

Ingredients:

    3 pears

    1 cup kale

    2 cups spinach

    1 cucumber

    ½ chard leaf

    1 cup snap peas

    ½ lemon

(Serves 2)

Directions:

1. Start by placing the kale, spinach, chard leaf, and snap peas into the blender.
2. Hand squeeze lemon juice for a ½ lemon directly into the blender and save the other half for later.
3. Peel the cucumber and cut into smaller pieces for easier blending before throwing into the blender as well.
4. Cut up all of the pears and mix in with the rest of the ingredients.
5. Blend them all until the all ingredients are mixed thoroughly.
6. Pour into glasses and serve.

My personal favorite ingredient in this juice is pear. These high in pectin fruits are not only rich in Vitamin B2, C and E but at the same time contain an abundant supply of copper, fiber and potassium. Pears work as both an antioxidant and an anti-carcinogen hence assisting in prevention heart disease and many cancers.

Apple Surprise

Ingredients:

2 granny smith apples

2 stalks of celery

1 spinach bunch

½ of a lemon

1 cucumber

1 slice ginger

¼ of a pineapple

(Serves 1)

Directions:

1. Hand-squeeze the juice of ½ a lemon and keep it aside. Save the other half of the lemon for later use.
2. Peel and cut up the pineapple into small chunks.
3. Next you can peel and cut up the apples, celery, cucumber, and ginger so that they can all fit into the blender or juicer better.
4. Place all of those ingredients into the blender along with the lemon juice, spinach, and pineapple. Spinach can be omitted if the ingredients are to be processed through a juicer.
5. Blend everything together until mixed well.

6. Chill the juice over some ice in glasses and serve.

We've all heard the saying about eating an apple a day, but combining apples with cucumber, spinach, pineapple and ginger is definitely as good as it gets. Not only is this juice amazingly effective in keeping your immune system strong but it also helps in keeping your heart healthy and prevents type 2 diabetes in the long run.

Beat the Heat

Ingredients

    2 parsley handfuls

    1" Ginger piece

    ½ cabbage

    2 apples

    1 lemon

    2 pears

    (Serves 1)

Directions:

1. Peel and cut the apples and pears up into small pieces and then place them into the blender.
2. Hand-squeeze the juice of the lemon and add it to the blender or cut it up in slices to run through the juicer along with other ingredients.
3. Place the rest of the ingredients into the blender and then turn it on at high speed. Recipe can be made juicer friendly by omitting the parsley leaves.
4. Blend until all of the ingredients are fully combined.
5. Pour the juice into a large glass and then enjoy!

Just like the name suggests, this juice is a must to ward off that dreadful summer heat. The Parsley not only improves digestion but it also helps your body fight various fungal and bacterial infections. The lemon and the ginger work wonders in curing migraines and sun strokes.

Conclusion

In conclusion, there is really not a good reason why everyone is not juicing every day. The health benefits are amazing and after just one week or so of enjoying these delicious juice recipes you will start to feel the changes in your health. These juice recipes will leave you feeling energized and refreshed without having to worry about putting together a big meal in order to get all the vitamins and minerals needed for a healthy body.

One of the immense health benefits of drinking fruit and vegetable juice regularly is that you will never have to worry about reaching the daily required amount of fruits and vegetables again. These juice drinks are designed to put all your daily servings of fruits and vegetables into an easy to swallow, tasty treat.

While these recipes are provided to get you started and give you some ideas, you don't have to follow any certain recipe book. It can be lots of fun to make up your own tasty combinations of various ingredients. What I have offered are just suggestions, you can easily substitute one ingredient for another to make your own customized juice drink. Juicing is a great and fun way to get healthy; everyone should try it for at least a week to a month and they are sure to feel like a new person in no time. Additives and preservatives have no place in human diet especially if we have an option or availability to use fresh ingredients. This book is intended to give the reader only a glimpse of the powerful nutrients packed into fruits and vegetables and just a little idea of the benefits they can provide upon becoming a part of our diet. This is also to know that the benefits listed are the more commonly known benefits of the ingredients and not all benefits of these ingredients can possibly be listed due to spacing and page limitations. The bottom line is, the idea of the book was to give the reader a rough overview of juicing and providing an easy opportunity to make their diet more healthy, natural, and preservative free. So keep it healthy, natural and unleash the Power of Juicing!!!!

CPSIA information can be obtained at www.ICGtesting.com
Printed in the USA
LVOW10s1609040115

421453LV00021B/479/P

9 781495 287671